New Zealand Wide

Moa
Beckett

Acknowledgements

The photographs in this book were supplied by:

Agrodome

Peter Bush

Focus New Zealand

Fotopacific

Helicopter Line

Hadden Lowrey

Barbara Todd

Cover – Lake Heron, with the Southern Alps in the background. Peter Bush
Endpapers – The sparkling waters and lovely hideaways of the Bay of Islands. Peter Bush
Title Page – The lighthouse at the tip of New Zealand, Cape Reinga. Peter Bush

ISBN 1-86958-124-5

© Moa Beckett Publishers Limited

Published in 1994 by Moa Beckett Publishers Limited
28 Poland Road, Glenfield, PO Box 100-749, North Shore Mail Centre, Auckland 1330

Printed through Bookbuilders, Hong Kong

NEW ZEALAND WIDE

The beginning of European settlement and the birth of photography both happened in the 1840s.
New Zealand, with its amazing sweep of scenic grandeur, seemed made for photography,
and the pioneer photographers of the past captured the emergence of a nation against
magnificent scenic backdrops. Heavy, cumbersome cameras gave way to the Box Brownies
and eventually the "point and shoot" cameras which nearly every tourist wears these days.
To travel round New Zealand and not record the stunning beauty of mountain and forest, lake and sea,
and the evocative interplay of light and shadow, is to miss one of the delights of touring this country.
From the sparkling blue waters of the Bay of Islands, to the magnificent snow-capped peaks of the
South Island; from the boom of surf on a wild West Coast beach to the lush dairy pastures of the
Waikato, from the thrill of Auckland Harbour busy with racing yachts to a golden autumn
countryside reflected in the mirror-like surface of Lake Hayes, the spectacular landscape offers
visual contrasts and experiences that are unique.
The land seems to beckon and issue a challenge to come and visit. Each time a traveller embarks on
a "panoramic saga" of New Zealand, the countryside promises the discovery of many more scenic spots.
This book is a record of many hours spent enjoying and photographing the natural beauty that is
New Zealand's heritage.

Early morning light on the Waitangi Treaty House,
built in 1833.

Boats, buildings and business – the Auckland city waterfront.

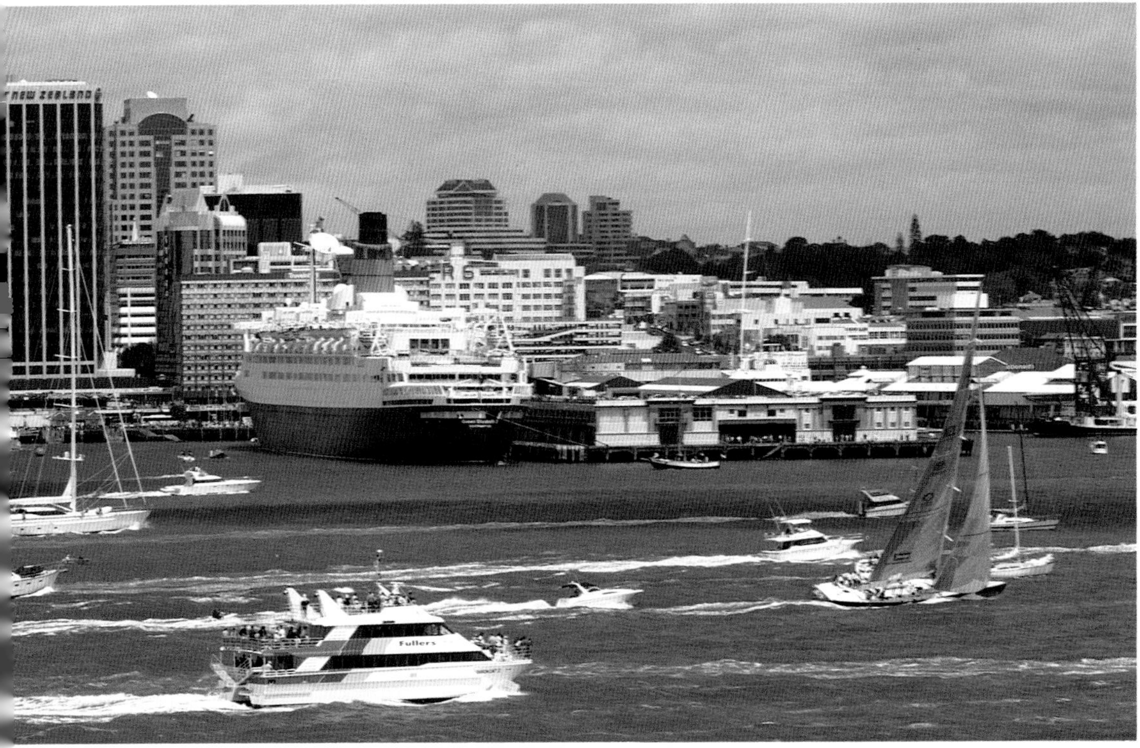

Focus New Zealand

A cruising shark at Kelly Tarlton's Underwater World, Auckland.

Auckland Museum, a landmark for miles around, with the Cenotaph on the left.

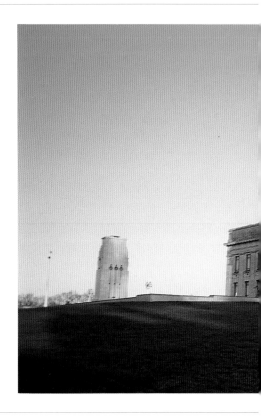

Intricate carvings with paua-shell-inlaid eyes adorn the buildings at Whakarewarewa Maori Village, near Rotorua.

A plume of boiling water erupts from Pohutu Geyser, Whakarewarewa.

Rotorua's Agrodome, featuring 19 breeds of
New Zealand sheep.

The Waikato River pours over the
spectacular Huka Falls.

Overleaf – Anglers line up in the waters of Lake Taupo
to catch the early morning sun and a few fish.   Hadden Lowrey

Looking across farmland to Mount Ruapehu,
with Mount Ngauruhoe on the left.

Overleaf – Mt Taranaki forms a perfect backdrop for
the blue waters of Lake Mangamahoe. Focus New Zealand

Gannets nesting at the sanctuary at
Cape Kidnappers.

Overleaf – A panoramic view of Wellington,
New Zealand's capital.

The *Aratika* interisland ferry steaming in
to berth at Picton.

Holidaymakers line the golden sands of
Kaiteriteri Beach.

A whale turns on a show for a group of whale
watchers off the Kaikoura Coast.

Overleaf – Victoria Square, Christchurch. Peter Bush

A breathtaking view of Christchurch by night from the top of Mt Cavendish.

The Church of the Good Shepherd on the shores of Lake Tekapo.

Overleaf – Mt Cook village with the majestic backdrop of Mt Sefton (left) and Mt Cook (centre back). Peter Bush

Sightseers fly in by helicopter to marvel at the frozen
beauty of the Franz Josef Glacier plateau.

Overleaf – The Fox Glacier cuts an icy path
through the mountains.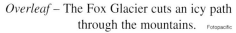

The cottages of early settlers still line the
main street of Arrowtown.

Overleaf – A leap of faith . . . a bungy jumper
takes flight from the Kawarau River Bridge. Peter Bush

Peter Bush

The "Lady of the Lake", TSS *Earnslaw*, steams across Lake Wakatipu with the craggy peaks of The Remarkables in the background.

The thrill of jet boating on the Shotover River, Queenstown.

Peter Bush

Riding high on the gondola to Bob's Peak (446 metres)
with Queenstown sprawled below.

Overleaf – Milford Sound, dominated by the
towering Metre Peak (centre left). Peter Bush

The deep, still waters of Doubtful Sound.

Previous spread – Trampers stop to enjoy the wild beauty of the MacKinnon Pass region of the Milford Track. Peter Bush

Hadden Lowrey

A brown kiwi searches for food – the nocturnal birds are a national symbol.

Overleaf – Mustering sheep in the tussocky expanses of the Mesopotamia area. Peter Bush